A Windy Day

by Lola M. Schaefer

Consulting Editor: Gail Saunders-Smith, Ph.D.

Consultant: Chris S. Orr, Certified Consulting Meteorologist, American Meteorological Society

Pebble Books

an imprint of Capstone Press
Mankato, Minnesota

Pebble Books are published by Capstone Press
818 North Willow Street, Mankato, Minnesota 56001
http://www.capstone-press.com

Library of Congress Cataloging-in-Publication Data
Schaefer, Lola M., 1950–
    A windy day/by Lola M. Schaefer.
    p. cm.—(What kind of day is it?)
    Includes bibliographical references and index.
    Summary: Simple text and photographs present a windy day, including what
the wind does and how people react to and use the wind for their various activities.
    ISBN 0-7368-0407-2
    1. Winds—Juvenile literature. [1. Winds.] I. Title. II. Series.
QC931.4.S33   2000
551.51′8—dc21   99-19438
                                                                    CIP

Note to Parents and Teachers

The series What Kind of Day Is It? supports national science
standards for units on basic features of the earth. The series also
shows that short-term weather conditions can change daily. This
book describes and illustrates what happens on a windy day. The
photographs support emergent readers in understanding the text.
The repetition of words and phrases helps emergent readers learn
new words. This book also introduces emergent readers to subject-
specific vocabulary words, which are defined in the Words to Know
section. Emergent readers may need assistance to read some words
and to use the Table of Contents, Words to Know, Read More,
Internet Sites, and Index/Word List sections of the book.

Table of Contents

A Windy Day 5
Kinds of Wind. 9
What Wind Does 13
How People Use Wind. 19

Words to Know 22
Read More 23
Internet Sites. 23
Index/Word List. 24

Today is a windy day.

Wind is the movement of air.

Light wind moves grasses.

Strong wind moves trees.

Clouds move quickly
on a windy day.

Seeds scatter
on a windy day.

Wet clothes dry
on a windy day.

People go sailing
on a windy day.

People fly kites
on a windy day.

Words to Know

air—the gases around the earth; we need air to breathe.

movement—the act of changing position from place to place; moving air goes from one place to another; this is wind.

scatter—to spread over a large area; wind scatters seeds over long distances.

seed—the part of a plant that can grow into a new plant

Read More

Davies, Kay and Wendy Oldfield. *Wind.* See for Yourself. Austin, Texas: Raintree Steck-Vaughn, 1996.

Grazzini, Francesca. *Wind, What Makes You Move?* I Want to Know. Brooklyn, N.Y.: Kane/Miller Book Publishers, 1996.

Owen, Andy. *Wind.* What Is Weather? Des Plaines, Ill.: Heinemann Library, 1999.

Internet Sites

Blustery Beginnings
http://sln.fi.edu/tfi/units/energy/blustery.html

Dan's Wild Wild Weather Page
http://www.whnt19.com/kidwx/index.html

From Windmills to Whirligigs
http://www.sci.mus.mn.us/sln/vollis/top.html

Index/Word List

air, 7
clothes, 17
clouds, 13
day, 5, 13, 15, 17, 19, 21
dry, 17
kites, 21
light, 9
movement, 7
people, 19, 21

quickly, 13
sailing, 19
scatter, 15
seeds, 15
strong, 11
today, 5
wet, 17
wind, 7, 9, 11
windy, 5, 13, 15, 17, 19, 21

Word Count: 53
Early-Intervention Level: 6

Editorial Credits
Martha E. H. Rustad, editor; Abby Bradford, Bradfordesign, Inc., cover designer; Heidi Schoof, photo researcher

Photo Credits
Cheryl A. Ertelt, 1
David F. Clobes, 4
Index Stock Imagery, Grantpix, cover
International Stock / Kirk Anderson, 12
Leslie O'Shaughnessy, 18
Shaffer Photography / James L. Shaffer, 8
Transparencies, Inc. / Henryk T. Kaiser, 14
Unicorn Stock Photos / Tom McCarthy, 10; Andre Jenny, 16; B. W. Hoffmann, 20
Uniphoto, 6